BLACK ROSE

by

Elijah Harmon

Copyright © 2017 L. Elijah Harmon
ISBN: 978-0997322514

All rights reserved. Names of individuals used in this book are fictional. This book or any portion thereof may not be reproduced or used in any manner whatsoever without the express written permission of the publisher except for the use of brief quotations in a book review.

Dedicated to my Grandmothers
Della Maye Soileau and Semonia Harmon

CONTENTS

Acknowledgments	I
Turn Back	1
Simple Desire	3
Making Thorns	5
Hermit Crab	7
Regina	9
Forever in Afghanistan	12
Warrior's Pain	14
Another Bottle Down	15
Regina's Love	17
A Rose Turned Black	19
5 o' clock	21
Everyone Knows	23
Re-up your Crazy	24
A Step to Grace	26
Downtown O City	28
Freedom of Mind	30
Jazz Tasting	32

Light Up	34
A Day in San Francisco	35
College Life Ends	37
The Call of Home	39
Night Shifted into Reality	41
Cloud of Doubt	42
What is next? A choice	44
Future of the Rose	46
Words of the Past	47

ACKNOWLEDGMENTS

Special thanks to my Mom and Dad, 2nd Platoon Charlie Co 1-508 PIR, my friends from Full Sail University, Dion and Sierra (my Writing Coach) at Destined Eloquence Publishing, and thank you Yolanda Jackson for giving me hope for my writing.

TURN BACK

Turn back the hands of time to when an innocent teen was ignorant to life beyond his surroundings.

Raised by God-Fearing parents in a household with two brothers.

Kept busy with football in high school and employment at a grocery store in his small, country town. That was all that he'd known life to be.

One day he would leave to embark upon a journey, traveling to a foreign land,
facing danger around each corner,
confronting situations where his life would be on the line.

Turn back the hands of time before his pure soul would tarnish from the sins that plagues the world.
Before fighting in war,
Before becoming stuck to a habit that could be fatal,
Before having to fix his broken heart from Regina's love.

A choice to leave the military life would lead to a great accomplishment.
A call for home would bring him back to where he left off.

Searching for a meaning in life, but looking back at the life already lived with a smile of no regret.
Met some of the most incredible people ever to know in life.
Overcame adversity when everything else seemed to have failed.
Traveled across the world and seen places that most people in his small, country town only witnessed on TV.

All made possible with something so simple,
An appetite for freedom, fed by pursuing such a path of mystery.

SIMPLE DESIRE

One day, a man dressed in uniform approached the innocent teen who was eager for a new life, asking for his service to the country.

With a desire to escape the normalcy of his idleness, he took the opportunity full-on without hesitation, leaving behind a monotonous rural life.

Embarking on a journey that was starting to become his new reality.

Without being exposed to the ways of the world, the seed of the rose was burrowed in foreign soil, watered by optimism, quenching its thirst for life, the seed now planted, ready to bloom.

Buried beneath the weight of all that was meant to stop the roses' growth, yet roots began to spout, creating a solid foundation.

The time was now for the rose to show the world what kind of rose it dreamt to be.

The will to reach the surface much stronger than what weighed it down.

Through resilience, a fresh rose pushed past the adversities, displaying superb beauty that all can marvel.

A simple desire has come to fruition and now the rose is ready for life.

MAKING THORNS

Long days spent in the scorching heat,
dripping with sweat.

Stuck out in the boonies where no signs
of life can be found.

Surrounded by pine trees underneath the
cover of humidity and few rain showers.

The way to here is by falling in from
the sky as the plane fly over,
carrying the bare essentials to survive,
weighing heavy on the back,
marching up and down hills that never
seemed to end,
fighting alongside your battle buddies,
shooting green dummies named Ivan
from sun up to sundown,
once it's all said and done,
pack up we're heading home,
everyone stands by until transportation
arrives in the next 20 minutes,
then leave out on the trucks.

Much rest is needed for the next time that
we roll out again.

Always training for war in the worst conditions,
learning how to fight an enemy who doesn't wear
a uniform,
fit for duty in maintaining physical strength
and mental awareness,
ready to execute with precision, accuracy, and
deadly force at any given notice,
obey orders from command that must be
completed precisely and in highest standards,
perform beyond the expectation of
being combat ready,
sufficient in the art of war and perfecting
improvisation,
all duties of all paratroopers who touches ground
at Fort Bragg.

Forging top notch warriors, thirsty for conflict,
for what lies ahead would be war.

Any ordinary man would find that a bit crazy, but
I found pride in being crazy in the eyes of regular
people.

HERMIT CRAB

Faced against an immoral lifestyle
attempting to impede,
the young warrior lies dormant in a shell,
witnessing wicked tendencies of those whom
surrounds his innocence.

He retreats to his innocent thinking, which was
carefully instilled during childhood,
having to come to terms with understanding the
drastic differences of life at home and life in
infantry.

In the shell, he remained to protect his virgin
mindset from aggressors seeking to destruct.

While everyone submerged into the culture that
consisted of drinking, strip clubs, fights, and
behaving nihilistically,
carried out by disregard for anyone's feelings.

Still, he disapproves and chooses to stands alone.

Trapped inside, new ideas begin to whisper,
thoughts of embracing this new kind of existence
began to become appealing,

indecisive between old traditions instilled within him at an early age,
or indulge into a new way of living that would be uncouth in the eyes of those who doesn't understand life in infantry.

A fierce battle would be fought.

In the end, defeat was inevitable.

A new era pushed through,
ushering in new ideas.

From the broken shell, arose a changed soul.

REGINA

When I first laid eyes upon Regina, time stopped,
everything going on around me didn't matter anymore,
she captured me with a sensual look that no man could glance away from.

There she was, sitting at bar waiting for me to make a move,
she wore a scarlet red dress,
her hair black as the midnight hour,
blue eyes mixed with green,
smooth tan skin,
a beautiful goddess who had come down from Olympias, blessing the world with her divine allure,
her essence made an eager young man gullible to do anything at her request.

Stuck in a daze with a body burning from desire, courage began marching,
the heart pounding so strong like King Kong beating on his chest,
sweat rolling down his forehead as if a small rainstorm had passed by,
fantasizing about how her lips would taste pressed against mine,

seeing the distance to Regina shrinking,
now is the time of bravery,
each footstep guided by confidence,
no stutter step of doubt can stop this force.

Regina knew his interest was there,
a little conversation wouldn't hurt.

Now all the tension is on him, attempting to impress a woman of such high caliber.

He took a seat right next to her and requested a drink.

Being a Southern gentlemen,
he asked "What's your favorite kind of poison?"

Wearing a charming smile, showing no teeth,
She replied with her sultry voice,
"Vodka and cranberry, if you don't mind."

Together they shared drinks and conversation.

"I see the want, but you don't have what it takes?" she asked.
"Have what it takes huh?" he asked, arrogantly.
blinded by passion, desperate thoughts emerged,
not wanting to let go of Regina, "Whatever it takes to be with you," he said, passionately.

she replied, "Well we have to see about that, now would we?"
From there, a curse manifested into fatal attraction.

A curse that would have him chasing after a woman who didn't considered the possibility of them being together, still she pretended to be interested.

The rose is poisoned.

FOREVER IN AFGHANISTAN

Days and nights spent looking back at times that
never seems to go away.
Always lurking in the shadows of the mind,
thoughts of anger, hate, pain, depression all
combined at once from all the violence brought
to our doorstep.

Images of bloodshed from friends and foes
constantly reappear in quiet moments,
lost in a trance of memories, time flow by
without notice, hours on end, thinking about the
firefights in the grape rows under
the hot sun, the verisimilitude of dying in
Afghanistan was a faith
one must come to terms with.

For soldiers in battlefield, there are no mistakes
that can be re done or fixed, always having to
pick a travel path, hoping not to get blown up or
walk into an ambush, only in conflict, will you
know what to do, hoping that it is the right
choice.

In war, true self emerges when in combat,

soon as those bullets start flying or those bombs
start blowing up, you either rise to the occasion
or freeze up with fear,
even a full-grown man can stall at
the moment of truth,
if you don't have common sense you're just as
good as dead,
if you are standstill, you may even pay in blood,
underestimate the enemy and
they will surely kill you,
trust the men who are on the left and right of you
and maybe you'll make it out,
we are not just fighting for the American people
but for the Afghans as well,
after the time is up, you can go home.

Apart of you will stay in war for the rest of your
life because your mind will remain there,
forever in hostile lands,
forever carrying the weight of battle,
forever in Afghanistan, my soul fights.

WARRIOR'S PAIN

As a Soldier,
We are trained for war,
Force to deal with harsh reality,
Perform beyond our normal ability,
Sacrifice our lives without question,
Accept death without quarrel,
Embrace every possibility,
Enforce every order,
Uphold a standard carrying pride,
Set an example for those to follow,
Glory is not our cause,
Pain is our acceptance,
Freedom is our outcome,
Sweat is our learning,
Blood is the price,
For our love of country, we fight,
A gift for you, whether you take it or not.

ANOTHER BOTTLE DOWN

Open the bottle,
Take a drink, the soul is thirsty for
the devil's nectar,
Time to slow down everything
going on around me,
Night's just beginning, good times ahead,
Hungry for more, can't stop now.

Fill the next glass,
Now we are getting somewhere,
Feeling the liquid fired going down,
Numbs the pain a little bit more,
Still there? Well I guess more is to come.

Another please,
Why am I still in touch with this pain?
It should be gone by now,
The pain is lingering around, but I'll fix that,
Let's see what you got!

No empty glass allowed,
Losing grip with myself, maybe I should quit,
Can't stand up, but I'll be damn if I let you win,
Pain, huh? I'll put you in the grave right next to
hope.

GIVE ME MORE!!!
You think you can just stay here?!
You have no idea who are messing with,
I'll drown you where you stand, you BASTARD.

Faded away,
You better not be here when I come back,
Tired of dealing with you,
Not enough liquor to rid you,
If the answer is in another bottle,
We will do this again.

REGINA'S LOVE

What is a loving relationship when only one person in the relationship loves the other?

Plenty of time spent chasing after a love that was supposed to be real, but instead it turned out to be fake,

Relentless efforts exhausted from constant refusal, but still he try to seek

Favor from a woman who did not care for him,

Seeing her being catered to by different men seared envy in him,

Standing from the shadows, he gazed on as he was neglected and forsaken by a goddess who seduced this desperate man into believing there was a chance.

A warrior emerges from the ashes of the battlefield,

Strong, gallant, and brave, all qualities of a champion,

Still this was not enough for Regina's love,

While others received it unconditionally,

Her love was something he always envisioned being in invested in,

Together forever until their dying days,

Ember of that fantasy lay cold with no fire to bare,

Regina's love towards him was empty and undetectable,

A curse that was designed to constantly pursue, but never to retrieve,

Oh, how Regina's love can damage even the strongest of men,

Her love left a scar on his heart that'll never be opened again.

A ROSE TURNED BLACK

Having face hideous conditions,
Destroyed by the viciousness that
corrupts the world,
A rose begins to die,
No tears to be wept,
Mercy is not shown,
Alone waiting to perish,
Vibrant red petals fall on the ground,
It cries out in pain, yet faced with silence,
Too weak to hold up,
Thirsty for purpose, but
Nothing around to quench,
Death seems inevitable,
In the hour of defeat,
A storm of meaning brews,
Hope rain downs,
Reviving life in the desolate soul,
A new rose arises.

Resilient to the brutality of which
reality can conflicted,
Confident that it can survive,
Fear is no longer a factor,
Tarnished by the enormity once experienced,
The pedals are stained black,
For the rose must convey the struggle,

That has been bestowed upon its life,
Thorns sharpen for foes,
To be met with opposition,
Preserving the beauty as other roses.

The black rose is ready to show the world,
That it can be strong and beautiful its' own way.

5 O' CLOCK

On a Friday evening, he and his friends
dressed up, looking good, smelling nice, and
eager to hit the town,
Head out for a night adventure with the hopes
of only having fun,
Kicking off the night with some fine Italian food
at a classy restaurant,
They knew that it was a fancy restaurant
By the luxury vehicles in the parking lot,
The customers having conversations about
European vacations and trips to Aruba,
They were just young soldiers out looking
for a good time,
No sense to brag about their small wages,
Watching the waitress serve whiskey, wine, and
German beer
To thirsty paratroopers who brought an appetite,
Stomachs full of pasta,
Still a lot of cash and time left on their hands,
Couple of cigars wouldn't do any harm
down at Anstead's,
An upscale, cool environment, made for cigar
enthusiast, filled with customers from all over
Latin America.

Everyone sipping on cocktails,

Puffing fine Dominican smoke,
Jazz music playing in the background,
A nice retreat away from work-related stress,
weighing heavy on the brain,
Just so we can laugh about it for the
sake of stability,
Dealing with the day to day life,
All boozed up, riding a tobacco high,
Wanting more nightlife to indulge in,
A gentlemen's club seemed like a perfect way to
end the night,
Victoria's was a fine club, where all drunk GIs
would hangout,
One that had his better judgment couldn't
help, but to smile and laugh,
At a bunch of intoxicated men spending money
on what couldn't be theirs'.

In the end,
Guys night out was meant to be that way, no
more no less.

EVERYONE KNOWS

Everyone knows,
The painstaking trip down Hardship Road,
A path of despair, doubt, and pain,
Never knowing when it will end,
Always reminiscing on the beginning
And dwelling in the present,
Where time seems endless,
We take the road many times,
Broken down,
Lost,
Lead astray,
Through it all,
We learn to navigate,
Every curve, stumbling block, and foggy view,
Although the end is not yet in view,
We take pit stops,
Refresh and Refit for more is to come,
The destination is closing in,
Almost there, can't stop now,
Not much longer until the end,
Arrival is a wonderful feeling,
Take a look back from where you came from,
Look where you are now,
One can never forget a trip down
Hardship Road.

RE-UP YOUR CRAZY

After five unforgettable years of war, training, jumping, and wearing the 82nd Airborne patch with a maroon beret, time was up,

Funny, those five years felt like they were long and slow, but now it seems as if it ended as soon as it began,

One minute, being 19 years young getting yelled at by a man, wearing a brown hat,

Next minute, jumping out of airplanes with back breaking equipment, training in the field by his 20th birthday,

In a 3rd world country, exchanging bullets with the enemy, playing a dangerous game of war,

Once there is time to reflect, 3 years have come and gone now he's a combat veteran at 21 years young,

Now having a chance to travel the country, touching coast to coast became a hobby,

Spending time with some amazing individuals,

After work, return to the barrack so that he and his battle buddies could have a good time together,

The Army made time for another deployment before he was thinking about getting out,

Combat operation wasn't in effect at this time, which made the new deployment seemed dull,

Returning home from the second trip, he was disappointed,

Age 23 with a mind made up that this was not for him anymore,

The final year with Uncle Sam went by in a blink of an eye,

Saying good bye to my brothers in arms was one of the hardest things to do,

24, joining the ranks of his father, being a veteran and on the way to college,

When asked, "Why didn't you reenlist?"

He answers, "The war was over so I got out."

A STEP TO GRACE

Here he come, rolling into the magic city, bringing a certain energy that only people from O Town can get a charge from,
High off the Florida sunshine like some hippie smoking Jamaican grass, flying in and out the clouds of joy hoping never to come down from the sky,
He feels welcome in the land that awaits his presence, driving by tall green palm trees lined up the sides of the roads,
Gorgeous Caribbean woman smile at the newly arrived Creole boy,
Restaurants, bars, art galleries, diversified cultures- all at his disposal,
Something that he never had at such capacity,
Captured by beauty and all Orlando had to offer,
Instant love would happen,
A type of love that everyone wishes you shut up about, but at the same time, you can't keep it to yourself,
A new life filled with promise, opportunity, and adventure that would shake the very foundation from what he was accustomed too,
Hitting the town with a serious blow of coolness that Miles Davis couldn't even deliver in a Championship Fight,

Hopping around, coming in and out bars
laughing, smoking, joking everyone around is
caught in the vibe,
Life was sweet as a cherry pie topped off with
whip cream ready to be served after dinner,
While the good times roll by not stopping
for rest,
New life style, ideas, brought about an awakening
of enlightenment,
This new way of thinking shattered old traditions
like a baseball going through a window,
Finally, being able to become the man that he
desired to be,
The world was better for him this way,
Sadly, he didn't know it was to be short lived.

DOWNTOWN ORLANDO

Hear that?

Sounds of music playing through the streets

Made for ears passing by,

Take a trip down to Tanqueray's, where a group

of young white guys who play instruments

just as good as old black blues musicians,

Rocking the small underground club,

So, everyone up top can feel it,

City folk going in and out of bars,

Drinking, smoking cigarettes, and hanging out,

Trying to hook up with other friends adding more life to the party,

Mixologist stick to a constant motion of shaking, pouring, handing, and raising,

Security being vigilante for the drunk idiots,

Skaters eating the pavement from failed kick flips landing with force,

Christians on the corner yelling at everyone, warning to repent,

Sweet Honey Barbecue from food stands seen across Church Street, responsible for the delicious aroma in the air,

Skyscrapers standing high and mighty casting down a sense of beautiful urban landscape,

City light brings a special look to the scene,

Helping the appeal for a wonderful night,

Grand Boeheim Hotel sitting on the corner

inviting all to come witness her glory,

No signs of theme parks around,

Just a place for the locals to unwind,

A downtown feeling waiting for anyone

Looking for a good time.

FREEDOM OF MIND

Sometimes a breath of fresh air in the new city
can change a man,
Take him away from his norm,
Put him in a place where the people are
down to earth,
Where new ideas are accepted,
Send him to college with an open mind
eager to learn,
What you will find is a man who's
been given perception,
The old folks back home would say, "My God!
The boy talking like a hippie,"
Has he come down with a slight case
of the liberal,
Didn't he served in the military, wearing fresh
haircuts, clean uniforms, and medals
pinned to his chest?
Wasn't he raised by parents who made
an honest living?
Why the sudden change ?
Freedom is what he tell them,
Freedom from strict guidelines created from
high-ranking officers,
Freedom from old rule customs and traditions
that are followed,
Freedom to be me without compromise,

Many would say he has been led astray,
Honestly,
Chains are finally broken and a spirit is
set free at last,
A bird released from captivity, ready to welcome
the sky on his own,
Who knew such a feeling existed by
a change of location,
How one chapter ends when the next one begins,
Shedding a new light on the world for fresh eyes
to see,
Why turn down the beautiful view for something
that has been seen already?
Freedom to have his own mind,
A mindset cannot be scripted nor
installed by others,
He finally feels that he is his own man,
Now free to be whoever he choose to be.

JAZZ TASTING

Laughter in the air,
People throwing back fine expensive drinks without a care in the world,
Wearing sharp clean suits and dresses hoping to land a companion by whispering sweet nothings in the ear,
He sat at the bar, covered down with a silver threaded suit, white satin shirt, black leather belt and shoes to match,
Drinking on some of Napa's finest, taking in some of the coolness that filled the joint,
In comes a beautiful Latin woman whose beauty sang across the room like sirens luring in sailors to their doom,
She had jet black hair, tan olive skin wearing ruby red lipstick, and a white dress that complement her natural curves, matched with pearl white heels to complete the look,
Women look on with envy while the men look with lust, but we continue the rhythm of the night,
The place is jumping, not skipping a beat, trumpet player laying down jazzy tunes that even the deaf can appreciate,
A midnight sanctuary away from the madness that plagued the streets of Orlando,

The vibe is captivating, everyone is drunk off the jazz and cool vibes,
The Mecca of chill,
Land of milk and honey for the beat generation to come back,
A young black woman takes the stage with demeanor of an innocent church girl, but had a voice that could make all the men howl,
The room was silent then comes the hit of piano followed by the roar of the trumpet,
Hear voice stormed into the hearts and souls of everyone in the club,
A reminisce of Billie Holiday,
Just another night at the Jazz Tasting.

LIGHT UP

Breathe in the marijuana smoke,
Keep the fire in my lung as a furnace,
Release the cloud for the sky to take,
May it rain down peace on earth,
Eyes open, though the lids are shut,
Body submerged in a pool of tranquility, leaving me soaking in heaven,
Ideas run wild like horses racing through fields,
Drift off to a land where there are no worries,
No pain, just a place of happiness for the soul to enjoy,
Ride the high like an old man in a Cadillac cruising on a Sunday evening,
Come down gracefully landing on both feet,
Finish with a feast of peanut butter, chocolate syrup, sliced bananas on wheat bread worth indulging,
There is nothing else left, but fade into the black now,
What a wonderful time that we had together again, Mary Jane.

A DAY IN SAN FRANCISCO

Blows through with a cool but delightful feeling,
waking him from a deep slumber,
I gazed his eye upon a beautiful
San Francisco day,
Taking a break from the hectic college life that
consumed him back in Orlando,
Travel to a place where you see the people make
haste with their busy lives,
While the homeless drift around with
no mind to care,
High off the Cali vibe, I was ready to take the day
without any fear in the world,
She calls out to him, "Be free from it all!"
He replied, "I'm yours for the taking."
Cruising around the elevated street taking in the
view, astonished by what she had to offer,
Bright colorful homes placed on the hillside,
Old fashioned buildings still in their heyday,
Tall skyscrapers that the eye can never miss,
Hear the Pacific waves crash on the rocky shores,
Made time to hang out with old hippies,
Reminiscing about bad acid trips down at
Haight & Ashbury,
Got a chance to rest my body on the soft grass,
Breathing in the sweet air of Dolores Park,
Come nightfall downtown lights up,

People from all backgrounds come to
fill the bars,
Hoping to drink their pain away,
Drinks and joints go up in the air,
Joy take the room without a fight,
Cali girls come out wearing their best outfits,
Trying to uphold their legendary title that the
world come to love,
It's a fun place made for those who seek
happiness,
Not a single moment of boredom,
Nothing but good times for everyone to enjoy
in the mystic city of San Francisco.

COLLEGE LIFE ENDS

Young and free with a little change in my pocket,
College life seemed to be on the up-and-up for the Creole kid,
Cutting strings away from past transgressions,
Old grudges that was held on with a tight grip loosened its' touch,
Smoking, joking, and making video games has never been something that I imagined while in the military,
Hey, college does know how to shed light on other concepts,
Gathering a group of strangers, some veterans, some fresh out high school, some trying to achieve something to show for,
Stuck together, forming a bond,
A union of friendship, made of hope,
Wonderful people from all over the states,
Chasing one dream,
All was well until time was up,
One after one, people began disappearing,
Doubt hungover like a storm cloud,
Raining out any type of bright sunshine on a beautiful day,
Watching all of it wash away in the blink of an eye,

Standing there soaking wet not knowing where to go now,
Why does it feel like good times leave so quick?
Bad times has a permanent residency one cannot evict,
Maybe someday he'll find balance,
Falling from grace hurts, but he always pick himself up,
He has been here before many times now,
True character comes out when the chips are down and you only have one more hit left,
But he'll show the world what kind of hand I'm holding,
So, he double down holding a straight poker face and play cards of triumph,
Before you know it, he walk away a degree, leaving competition baffled and confused,
Now he has achieved something that he never imagined of getting.

THE CALL OF HOME

Years have gone by, living a life filled with
exciting adventures,
Going to Afghanistan twice and returning back
home each time without shedding
a single drop of his blood,
Traveling around the United States and Europe,
experiencing new cultures and
visiting different cities,
Contract was up in the army, it was time to get an
education using the benefits so rightfully earned,
Home was calling, longing for
rest and decompression,
Sadly, the call was ignored, but faith would have
it call again when the time seem right,
Going down to Florida would be an eye-opening
journey in hopes of a new future, the challenge
would be accepted,
Pursing the path of a Game Designer was
vigorous, but rewarding,
Facing a different kind of adversary where it
wasn't someone trying to kill him,
This time, his adversaries were balancing
homework, programming, and transitioning back
into the civilian world,
Just when it felt like it was time to quit, his
strength was renewed for a big push, wanting to

finish what I started,
Through the help of friends, instructors, and
tutors, a goal was reached,
Eternally grateful for encountering such great
people once again in his life,
In the moment of victory, a call from home came
through requesting his presence,
Finally, it was the time to go home,
Plans for the next adventure would need
money and reflection,
for a new lesson would be taught and in it would
be patience.

NIGHT SHIFTED TO REALITY

Surrounded by the metal and concrete jungle, my thoughts run wild,
Looking around in hopes to find a better future,
Watching time move slow like sap
rolling down a tree,
Days come together like one big blur, not knowing which one to recognize,
The sun is a stranger who lets me know that my day is over,
The moon is my friend who call for my duty,
Sleeping while awake in purgatory,
The mind lays in idle,
Trapped in a world where I'm not the protector,
The shepherd whose flock turned against,
The wolf stares waiting to attack,
Good memories play back and forth, stuck on repeat,
Fast forward the times of pain that felt so long yet quite frequent,
Soon paradise will come to bask in with joy,
All that has been forbidden will be for the taking,
Patience is the virtue and fortune is the prize,
Those who sacrifice will triumph
Others fold when adversity comes with force.

CLOUD OF DOUBT

Sitting Back.
Watching the big wings excited with big
smiles across their faces,
Going home with a look of relief,
Meanwhile, a young creole boy face yells
tired, grumpy, and broke without uttering a single word,
He clocks on for an another long shift,
Just some poor soul trying to make a buck.

Struggle.
Gray skies capture the feeling that lingers around,
Bringing back memories from old crappie days that
came before,
Reminding him that times are stuck between
happiness and depression.

Remise.
He dig deep, wiping the sweat from my eyes,
Working in the hot Cajun sun, trying to bury self-pity
on top of angry,
Drinking a glass of false motivation to cool down,
Every sip quenches the thirst for hope, only leaving him
to ask for more.

Endure.
Where is this all heading to?
When will it end?
Why am I doing this?
Was it a mistake to return home?
Questions echoing in his empty mind,

No answer to fill the vacancy,
Like an apartment with no tenant.

Doubt.
All about paying dues is what the old folks say,
Words of wisdom from the ones who been around,
Seasoned veterans of the game called life,
Willing to share their knowledge,
A golden life lesson can be taught,
If the young can listen long enough,

Advice.
This all too familiar to him,
He feels as if he's been here before,
Conquered over many obstacles in his young exciting life,
Defeated multiple challenges in some of the worst conditions,
"Who am I to be down like some old bum?" He ask.

Strength.
Reminded of triumph, the soul is revived,
Energy rejuvenated by passion flowing
through the veins,
Confidence is restored from overcoming self-loathing
mixed with hate,
The long vigorous road will end,
He'll be the one to finish.

WHAT IS NEXT? A CHOICE

Life is filled with different journeys that
we all must take,
Many choices are presented, but he must choose
the best choice for him,

Where to go? What to Do? How to do what is
chosen? All questions in need of answers,

One has traveled down numerous roads at such a
young age,

Yet, he still return to the point of origin,

At home, plans are to assemble,

For the search of destiny draws near,

The future can look so bright for the optimistic
who seeks prosperity and good fortune,

A fantasy worth chasing in the eyes of a man,
carrying great determination,

Be warned,

The past leaves caution for the hasty hopeful,

Take noticed of the hazards that lie ahead because they can stop you,

Walk vigilante through the unknown lands, be wise,

After all you have been through,

Use your experience to your advantage, keeping in mind of wisdom learned,

Everything else is taken into consideration while the rest is out of your control,

Therefore, a new purpose awaits and in it lies a chapter in the book of life.

FUTURE OF THE ROSE

After stunning the world with
unique beauty and perseverance,
The black rose distinguishes itself in a manner of
great dignity,
Not ashamed of its' eccentric appearance that
some may deem unfit,
Nor will feel alienated because a rose still stands
amongst the other roses as one of their own,
Carrying a familiar demeanor while displaying a
distinct attraction which many admire,
Nevertheless, the future look so bright for a rose
that has been stained by the ugliness of the
world,
Through it all, the black rose retained the same
mystique and integrity
without changing completely,
Driven by passion and desire, the black rose
stands ready to be contested by adversity,
Even though the rose's pigmentation has change,
Its character holds a great sense of pride for it
has proven itself worth in the eyes of critics,
Time will tell how long the Black Rose will last or
how far it will grow,
No matter what, it has made its place in the
world that no one can ever take away.

WORDS OF THE PAST

Lying in bed, holding on to conscience, fading into sleep,
Voices begin to speak,
Broken dreams from the past whisper in the ear,
Every mistake in life begins preaching sermon,
Relying a message to be heeded,
All attention is focused,
Old aspirations speak of caution in a way the elderly speak to the young,
Warning him, the lessons that have learned must be applied,
Those who forget are destined for a life of repeat,
Forever in a perpetual loop,
Better to stop and listen with an open mind,
Rather than pay dearly by being stuck in old ways,
Pride can be death,
Push to be humble,
May I accept such grateful wisdom given by previous mistakes,
Life's teaching will continue to guide his path.

www.ingramcontent.com/pod-product-compliance
Lightning Source LLC
LaVergne TN
LVHW051711080426
835511LV00017B/2862